Dedicated to my boys,
Logan and cal.

May you never give up
on your dreams.

www.mascotbooks.com

BE A BIG HERO

For more information, please contact:
Mascot Books
620 Herndon Parkway #320
Herndon, VA 20170
info@mascotbooks.com

Library of Congress Control Number: 2019917056

CPSIA Code: PRTWP0720A
ISBN-13: 978-1-64543-236-4

Printed in South Korea

BE A
BIG HERO

Jennifer Bacon

illustrated by Lara calleja

What's wrong with
this ocean scene?

Its coral reefs are not
so pretty and clean.

Look at all this cluttering debris.

What happened to our beautiful sea?

Every fish and animal
Play a special role,

To keep the Earth's balance
healthy and whole.

We need our oceans to stay intact.

It's important for our planet, and that's a fact.

It goes to the landfill, out of sight,

But ends up in the sea which isn't right.

These floating wrappers
  from our treats

Are made of plastic
  which we do not eat.

But the ocean animals
don't know better

It looks like food to
them, just wetter.

This plastic and trash won't go away.

For hundreds of years these wrappers will stay.

Plastic is so durable and strong,

which makes its journey terribly long.

Plastic gets stuck in our ocean friends' tummies,

Making them feel icky and crummy.

Then they can't digest the food they need.

"Washed Up On Shore" the headlines read.

But it's not just the sea that is affected
Other bodies of water are also infected.

Litter makes its way into
lakes and down the rivers

And poses danger to the
amazing marine critters.

But don't get too down or feel too sad,

There's so much we can do
    to conquer this bad.

We can all be big heroes and
    we can always help.

We can save all the animals that
    swim through the kelp!

When we are out and about,
we need not litter.

We need not use that pesky
plastic and glitter.

Our friends of the sea need a clean home,

So they can thrive, live, and roam!

we can start by buying fewer
plastic goods at the store.

carrying groceries in reusable
bags is not such a chore.

keep the contents of
your garbage low.

Reuse, compost, recycle,
and you'll be a pro!

Thankfully, there are many
   alternatives to plastic,

compostable bamboo toothbrushes
   work just as fantastic.

We should let restaurants
   and companies know

Their customers want plastic-
   free products and cargo!

We need to be more aware of
the problems we cause,

Reduce our pollution, single-
use plastic, and straws.

Don't get discouraged,
it takes a while,

To make new habits
or a new lifestyle.

We have to keep the
main goal in mind,

Saving and showing our ocean
creatures we can be kind.

Amazing marine creatures like sea
turtles, dolphins, and whales

Are in danger of just being
in books and old tales.

we can all be protectors
of the ocean and land,

we owe it to the animals
to take a stand.

So we can live on this
planet and always see

The beautiful creatures
that live in our sea!

TIPS TO CUT DOWN ON PLASTIC POLLUTION

- Make efforts to lower what your family sends to the landfill.
- Repurpose items. Find a new purpose for something instead of tossing it.
- Recycle. Glass and cans are easier to recycle than plastic.
- Buy fewer plastic products and plastic-wrapped foods.
- Use fewer single-use items like foil, napkins, coffee cups, etc.
- Repair broken items and mend clothing instead of tossing.
- Donate unwanted toys, clothes, and household items.
- Compost food scraps, used coffee grounds, soiled cardboard boxes, and more.
- Take containers to the restaurant for leftovers to avoid single-use containers.
- Switch from plastic single-use water bottles to reusable water bottles.
- Bring reusable bags and produce bags to the store instead of using plastic bags.
- Recycle any plastic bags you do have to the stores that take them.
- Follow recycling rules.

Keep garbage out of the recycling bin. Recyclables should be washed or cleaned. Materials should be separated. Items that consist of more than one material do not get recycled.

Do not litter and encourage others to avoid littering.

Keep a garbage bag in your car for when there isn't a garbage can around. Encourage others to also refrain from littering. Come across litter outside? Be a big hero and pick it up!

Make choices that are better for the environment.

Support farmers' markets, bulk sections, and plastic-free products. Support businesses and companies that make efforts to keep their footprint small, and whose mission it is to help the environment and the ocean. Donate to non-profits that support and protect wildlife.

Teach children to have respect for the Earth and its creatures.

Pick up trash when out on walks or adventures with your kids. It may not be your trash, but it is your planet! Show children that we need nature and that nature also needs us.

Practice until it's a habit! It gets easier to remember with more practice!

Please help support my non-profit of choice: The Ocean Cleanup.

Portions of the proceeds for this book will go to this amazing organization!

www.theoceancleanup.com

www.mrsbossybacon.com

@mrsbossybacon

About the Author

Jen Bacon has always had a passion for nature and the creatures in it. Growing up near the Puget Sound and the mountains in Washington State, water and nature was never far away. With a deep desire to help the animals affected by pollution, she started finding ways to make a difference. Her husband Sean and her sons, Logan and Cal, have joined her efforts in protecting the animals that live with us, starting with changing their lifestyle to be more eco-friendly. *Be a Big Hero* is her first book and was originally written for her sons, but her dreams were to teach future generations about the impacts of plastic pollution. She is currently working on her second children's book about climate change. You can follow her efforts at mrsbossybacon.com, and on Twitter, Instagram, and Facebook at @mrsbossybacon.